CW01502446

What is the DASH Diet?

It's a diet and eating style that was conceived by the NHLBI (National Heart, Lung and Blood Institute) with the goal of decreasing high blood pressure.

DASH stands for Dietary Approaches to Stop Hypertension and in addition to lowering blood pressure, the diet has also been shown to help prevent cancer, heart disease, diabetes, osteoporosis and strokes.

The DASH diet is a healthy and well-balanced diet with its main focus being on low sodium consumption. Greatly reducing, or removing, ones intake of sodium has been shown to be highly effective in the lowering of blood pressure.

Followers of the DASH diet also tend to lose fat at an accelerated rate. As the DASH diet is built around the consumption of whole grains, fruits, vegetables and proteins it is excellent for those looking to lose fat without sacrificing their favourite foods.

However the DASH diet isn't only for those wishing to lower their blood pressure or lose weight, it is actually an excellent diet for anyone looking to live a healthy life. The US government stated that the DASH Diet is an "exemplary way" for people of all ages to eat.

It was also rated by the US News and World Report as the best dietary approach available. It has now won this award 4 years in a row.

So, whether you're looking to lower your blood pressure, lose weight or just be healthier the DASH Diet is probably the perfect choice for you and your family.

Don't Forget to Get Your Free Gift

As my way of saying "thanks for buying" I've put together a free gift for you:

www.GoodLivingPublishing.com/dashchicken

Visit the link above to download now.

Contents

DASH Foods

You might be curious as to what foods you can eat whilst following the DASH diet so I've put together this short section to answer that question.

Given the title of this book you've probably guessed that fish and seafood are allowed whilst following DASH, but what are the other foods?

- Whole Grains

- Fruit

- Vegetables

- Dairy, but limit your intake

- Poultry

- Lean beef

- Legumes and beans

- Nuts, but limit your intake

- Oils, use extra-virgin olive oil

Given the range of foods you are allowed to eat whilst following the DASH diet you should have no problems incorporating it into your life.

Always remember that when buying products check to make sure they are low-sodium/low-salt.

Now we've briefly covered a bit of background on the DASH diet it's time to dive into what you bought this book for... the recipes.

Every recipe in this book is packed full of flavour, easy to cook and DASH diet allowed, I know you're going to love cooking these fish and seafood meals.

The DASH Fish & Seafood Recipes

Scallop & Veg Skewers

Makes 2-3 Servings.

Ingredients

1 lb. of scallops

1 tbsp olive oil

Juice from half of a lemon

½ tsp thyme

2 shallots, peeled and halved

2 bell peppers, cut into thick chunks

6 cherry tomatoes

½ zucchini, cut into chunks

Ground black pepper, to taste

Skewers, soaked in water

Directions

In a bowl combine the oil, lemon juice, thyme and pepper. Mix well before adding the scallops and covering. Leave the scallops in the marinade for 20 minutes.

Whilst the scallops marinade preheat your broiler/grill.

Skewer the vegetables and scallops in an alternating fashion.

Season with pepper.

Place under the heat source and cook for about 3 minutes per side.

Red Onion Salmon

Makes 4 Servings.

Ingredients

4 salmon fillets

3 cloves of garlic, minced

2 red onions, finely chopped

2 tbsp olive oil

2 tsp ground cayenne

1 cup of uncooked brown rice

Directions

Preheat your oven to 375F.

Cook the rice according to the package instructions. Whilst the rice cooks move onto the next step.

In a bowl mix together the garlic and onion.

Take a large baking dish and lay out the red onion along the bottom creating a base layer.

Sprinkle 1 tsp of the cayenne over the onion and then lay the salmon fillets, skin side down, onto the onion.

Drizzle the olive oil over everything and then sprinkle the remaining cayenne over the dish.

Cover and put in the oven for 18-20 minutes.

Serve the salmon over the cooked rice and use the juices from the dish as a sauce.

Pineapple Marinated Salmon

Makes 2 Servings.

Ingredients

2 salmon fillets

½ cup pineapple juice

2 cloves of garlic, minced

1 tsp soy sauce

¼ tsp ground ginger

¼ tsp sesame oil

Ground black pepper, to taste

1 cup of chopped pineapple

½ cup of couscous

Directions

Mix together the pineapple juice, garlic, soy sauce and ginger in a bowl.

Place the salmon fillets on a plate and pour the pineapple juice mixture over the top. Cover, transfer to the refrigerator and let marinade for 2 hours. Turn every 30 minutes.

Preheat your oven to 375F.

Cook the couscous according to the package instructions.

Whilst the couscous cooks take a small baking dish and lay out the salmon fillets on it. Drizzle with the sesame oil and season with black pepper.

Add the chopped pineapple to the dish then cover and bake for 15-20 minutes.

Serve the salmon over the couscous and use any juices left over in the dish as the sauce.

Honey Scallops

Makes 4 Servings.

Ingredients

1 lb. of scallops

4 tbsp honey

2 tbsp lime juice

3 tbsp olive oil

2 bell peppers, chopped

1 onion, chopped

1 courgette, chopped

2 cups of spinach

Directions

Preheat your broiler/grill. Position the rack around 4-5" from the heat source.

Lay foil over a baking tray and grease with 1 tbsp of olive oil.

Add the honey, lime juice and 1 tbsp olive oil to a bowl, whisk together.

Add the scallops and gently toss to coat. Leave to marinade for 5 minutes.

Place a pan over a medium heat and add the remaining olive oil. Once the oil is heated add the onion, courgette and peppers, cook for 5 minutes stirring frequently.

Add the spinach to the pan and cook for a further 2 minutes. Take off the heat and set aside.

Lay the scallops out on the baking sheet and then place under the heat for 4 minutes. Turn and then cook for a further 2 minutes.

Serve up the vegetables and lay the scallops over the top. Pour the remaining juices over the dish as a sauce.

Shrimp & Spring Vegetables Stir Fry

Makes 4 Servings.

Ingredients

1 block of noodles, around 8 oz.

1 cup of baby shrimp

2 tbsp sesame oil

1 tbsp grated fresh ginger

2 cloves of garlic, minced

2 tbsp soy sauce

1 cup of broccoli florets

1 cup of bean sprouts

8 cherry tomatoes, halved

1 cup chopped spinach

2 scallions, finely chopped

1 tbsp red chilli flakes

Directions

Add the noodles to a pot filled with water and bring to the boil. Cook for 12 minutes, or according to package instructions.

Drain the noodles and set aside.

Place a large pan over a medium-high heat and add the sesame oil. Once the oil is heated add the shrimp, the ginger and the garlic, cook for 3 minutes.

Add the broccoli and soy sauce. Cook for 4 minutes, stirring frequently.

Add the noodles and the remaining vegetables, toss and cook for 4-5 minutes.

Take off the heat, sprinkle in the chilli flakes and toss.

Simple Seabass

Makes 4 Servings.

Ingredients

4 Seabass fillets

4 tbsp lemon juice

2 tsp garlic, minced

2 tsp Italian seasoning

Ground black pepper, to taste

8 stalks of asparagus, ends removed

1 onion, roughly chopped

1 tbsp olive oil

Directions

Preheat your oven to 375F.

Lay out a square of foil on a baking tray. Using ¼ of the onion create a bed on the foil.

Place 1 fillet of Seabass on the onion then lay the asparagus over the fish.

Season with 1 tbsp of the lemon juice, ½ tsp of garlic. ½ tsp of Italian seasoning, black pepper and a drizzle of olive oil.

Wrap up the foil around the fish creating a sealed package.

Repeat this with the remaining 3 fish fillets until you have 4 packages.

Bake in the oven for 20-25 minutes. The Seabass should flake easily with a fork.

Pine Nut Crusted Cod

Makes 4 Servings.

Ingredients

4 pieces of cod

½ cup of pine nuts

2 tbsp of olive oil

2 tbsp of pesto

12 baby potatoes, cut into slices

1 onion, roughly chopped

1 courgette, chopped

Ground black pepper, to taste

Directions

Preheat your oven to 350F.

Add the pine nuts, pesto and olive oil to a bowl and mix well.

Lay the potatoes, courgette and onion out on an oven proof dish. Season with black pepper.

Place the cod pieces onto the vegetable mixture.

Coat the cod in the pine nut and pesto mixture. If any is left over then add it to the vegetables. Season with more black pepper.

Cover and bake in the oven for 18 minutes. Remove the cover and bake for a further 4-5 minutes uncovered.

Fettuccine Clams

Makes 4-6 Servings.

Ingredients

10 oz. fettuccine

3 tbsp minced garlic

2 large tomatoes, chopped

2 cups of frozen corn kernels

½ cup of dry white wine

1 tbsp olive oil

4 tbsp chopped basil

8 oz. of clams

Ground black pepper, to taste

Directions

Cook the pasta for 8-10 minutes (or according to package instructions) in a pot filled with boiling water. Drain and set aside.

Place a pan over a medium heat and add the olive oil.

Once the oil is heated add the garlic, the tomatoes, the corn and the wine. Stir well and then add the basil. Cover and bring to the boil stirring occasionally.

Reduce the heat to low and add the clams. Cook for 1-2 minutes before adding the pasta.

Toss well to mix everything together then cook for 2-3 minutes, or until the pasta is warmed through.

Season with black pepper before serving.

Halibut in a Spiced Salsa

Makes 4 Servings.

Ingredients

4 fillets of halibut

2 large tomatoes, diced

2 tbsp basil, chopped

1 tsp oregano, chopped

1 tbsp minced garlic

3 tsp of ground paprika

3 tsp olive oil

1 bag of mixed salad

Directions

Preheat your oven to 350F.

Grease a baking tray with 1 tsp of olive oil and set aside.

Mix together the tomato, garlic, paprika, oregano, olive oil and basil in a bowl.

Lay the fish out on the baking tray and spoon the tomato mixture over each fillet.

Place in the oven and bake for 13-15 minutes.

Serve with a mixed salad.

Halibut with a Pea Puree

Makes 2 Servings.

Ingredients

2 halibut fillets

5 oz. of frozen peas

1 & ½ tsp basil

Ground black pepper, to taste

½ tsp olive oil

8 baby potatoes, chopped

2 tbsp of olive oil

Directions

Preheat your oven to 400F.

Let the peas defrost and then add to a blender, along with the basil and pepper. Pulse until smooth.

Place a pan over a low heat. Add the pea puree and heat whilst stirring occasionally.

Place another pan over a medium-high heat and add the olive oil. Place the fish, skin side down, in the pan and cook for 2 minutes.

Carefully remove from the pan, add to a baking dish and place in the oven for 8 minutes.

Whilst the fish is cooking add the chopped potatoes to the pan and sauté for 8 minutes, tossing frequently. Season with black pepper.

Serve the pea puree drizzled over the fish and potatoes, season with more pepper to taste.

Parmesan Crusted Salmon

Makes 2 Servings.

Ingredients

2 salmon fillets

2 oz. of sour dough bread

½ cup of grated parmesan

1 clove of garlic, minced

1 tbsp chopped basil

1 tsp olive oil

½ tbsp balsamic vinegar

1 tbsp olive oil for greasing

Directions

Preheat your oven to 450F.

Add the bread to a food processor and pulse until it is reduced to fine bread crumbs.

Next add the parmesan, garlic, basil, 1 tsp of olive oil and the balsamic. Process until well combined.

Using the remaining olive oil grease a baking dish. Lay the salmon on the baking dish and coat each fillet in the blended mixture.

Cook for 18-20 minutes in the oven.

Salmon in Caper Sauce

Makes 4 Servings.

Ingredients

4 salmon fillets

½ cucumber, seeded but not peeled

½ cup of non-fat Greek yogurt

1 tbsp capers

1 tbsp oregano

1 onion, thinly sliced

Ground black pepper, to taste

1 tsp paprika

2 tsp olive oil

Directions

Grate the cucumber then place in a bowl along with the Greek yogurt, capers, oregano, green onion and black pepper. Mix everything well.

Lay out the salmon fillets and sprinkle with the paprika.

Place a pan over a high heat and add the olive oil.

Add the salmon, skin side down, and cook for 6 minutes before flipping and cooking for another 5 minutes.

Serve the salmon with cooked green vegetables and the caper sauce drizzled over everything.

Tuna & Black Bean Salad

Makes 2 Servings.

Ingredients

1 tin of tuna, drained

1 can of black beans, drained and rinsed

1 bag of mixed salad leaves

1 bell pepper, chopped

1 tsp of ground cayenne

1 tsp of ground paprika

2 tbsp of olive oil

2 tbsp of hot sauce

Directions

Add all the ingredients to a large bowl and mix everything well.

Maple Glazed Salmon

Makes 4 Servings.

Ingredients

4 salmon fillets

¼ cup of maple syrup

1 clove of garlic, minced

¼ cup of balsamic vinegar

Ground black pepper, to taste

1 tbsp of olive oil

Parsley for garnish

Directions

Preheat your oven to 375F.

Coat a baking tray with 1 tbsp of olive oil and set aside.

Place a small pan over a medium heat and add the maple syrup, balsamic and garlic. Mix well and cook for 1 minute. Take off the heat and split the sauce in two.

Place the salmon, skin side down, on the baking tray and brush with the maple sauce. Bake for 5 minutes and then baste with more sauce. Repeat this process until the fish is cooked through, around 18-20 minutes.

Once salmon is cooked use the remaining maple glaze as the sauce. Garnish with parsley and serve.

Flaked Fish in Lemon Lentils

Makes 2 Servings.

Ingredients

2 oz. of lentils, Puy are best

½ onion, finely chopped

½ carrot, finely chopped

1 celery stick, finely chopped

½ pint of vegetable stock

1 tbsp low-fat crème fraiche

1 tbsp chopped dill

The zest of ½ a lemon

2 white fish fillet, you can use any white fish for this recipe

Handful of baby spinach

Directions

Add lentils into an oiled pan with the chopped onion, carrot and celery and place over a medium heat.

Add the stock and bring to the boil. Stir a few times and reduce the heat. Cover and let simmer for 20-25 minutes. The lentils should be tender after this time.

In a bowl mix together the crème fraiche, half the dill and the lemon zest, adding a little seasoning, to taste.

Put the fillets in a shallow microwave proof dish with a splash of water and cover with cling film leaving one corner open slightly.

Microwave on medium for 4-6 minutes until the fish flakes easily when touched with a fork. Flake the fish with a fork.

Once the lentils are tender, add the spinach and stir. Continue to cook at a low heat and add the crème fraiche once the spinach has wilted.

Serve and top with flaked fish. Garnish with the remaining dill.

Seafood Linguine

Makes 2 Servings.

Ingredients

Handful of linguine pasta

1 tsp of minced garlic

4 cherry tomatoes, quartered

2 egg yolks

1 can of tinned crab meat

2 handfuls of frozen shrimp

3 tbsp olive oil

2 tsp red pepper flakes or dried chilli flakes

Ground black pepper, to taste

Directions

Cook the linguine in a pot of boiling water for 8-10 minutes or, according to instructions on package.

Whilst the linguine cooks place a pan over a medium heat and add 1 tablespoon of oil.

Add the tomatoes, shrimp, pepper flakes and garlic to the pan and stir well. Cook for 3 minutes, stirring frequently, before adding the crab meat and egg yolks.

Cook for another 2 minutes, stirring continually.

Drain the linguine and add to the pan. Toss well.

Drizzle the remainder of the oil on the pasta and season with pepper.

Stuffed Sole

Makes 2 Servings.

Ingredients

2 sole fillets

2 tsp olive oil

2 cups of spinach leaves

2 tsp minced garlic

Ground black pepper, to taste

½ tsp butter, melted

1 cup of risotto

Directions

Preheat your oven to 400F.

Cook the risotto according to package instructions.

As the risotto cooks coat a baking dish with 1 tsp of olive oil and set aside.

Place a pan over a medium heat and add the remaining olive oil. Add the spinach, garlic and pepper to the pan, cook for 3 minutes.

Lay out the sole fillets on the baking dish and spoon the spinach mixture onto the fish. Roll up the fillets so the spinach is trapped inside.

Brush the top with the butter and then bake in the oven for 10 minutes.

Serve the sole on top of the cooked risotto. Pour any remaining juices from the baking dish over the risotto.

Lemon Swordfish

Makes 4 Servings.

Ingredients

4 swordfish fillets

2 lemons, quartered

1 tbsp sugar

½ tsp olive oil

½ tsp chopped garlic

¼ cup of chopped parsley

Directions

Preheat your oven to 375F.

Mix together the lemon wedges and sugar in a bowl.

Add the lemons to a baking dish, cover and cook for 55-60 minutes.

Switch your oven to the broiler and position the rack 4-5" away from the heat source.

Place the swordfish fillets on a baking tray, drizzle the oil over it and top with the garlic.

Cook for 5 minutes before turning and cooking for a further 5 minutes.

Before serving squeeze the sugared lemon wedges over the swordfish. Sprinkle with the parsley and serve.

Blueberry Seabass

Makes 4 Servings.

Ingredients

4 Seabass fillets

1 & ½ cups of blueberries

¼ cup of chopped sage

Ground black pepper, to taste

1 cup garlic of croutons, crushed

1 tsp orange zest

2 tbsp orange juice

1 tbsp olive oil

Directions

Mash together the blueberries with 1 tsp of the sage. Season with pepper and set aside.

In a separate bowl mix together the croutons, the remaining sage, the orange peel and season with pepper. Mix well then add the orange juice and olive oil.

Preheat your broiler/grill and move the rack 4-5" below the heat source.

Place the fish, skin side up on the rack and cook for 5 minutes. Flip the fish over and top with the crouton mixture. Cook for a further 3-5 minutes.

Serve with the blueberry sauce over the top of the crusted fish.

Makes 4 Servings.

Ingredients

4 halibut fillets

Cooking spray

2 tbsp unsalted butter, melted

¾ cup of chopped hazelnuts

1 cup of mixed berries

½ tsp sugar

Directions

Preheat your oven to 400F.

Grease a baking tray with cooking spray or use olive oil.

Brush the fish with butter and then gently rub the chopped nuts onto both sides.

Once well coated place the fillets on the greased baking pan.

Cook for 9-10 minutes.

As the fish is cooking pulse the berries in a blender for 1-2 minutes. Pass the puree through a fine-mesh sieve to remove any seeds and pulp. Stir the sugar into the sieved fruit sauce then warm in a small pan.

Serve the sauce over the fish and with a side of green vegetables.

Dill Seabass

Makes 4 Servings.

Ingredients

4 Seabass fillets

1 & ½ tbsp onion, chopped

1 tsp capers

1 & ½ tsp chopped fresh dill

1 tsp Dijon mustard

1 tsp lemon juice

1 lemon, for squeezing

Directions

Preheat your oven to 375F.

Mix together the capers, mustard, dill, chopped onion and lemon juice in a small bowl.

Lay out 4 squares of foil on your work surface and place a fillet on each. Squeeze lemon juice over each fillet of fish. Spoon the dill mixture onto the fish and spread evenly.

Wrap the foil around each fillet creating individual packages.

Bake in the oven for 12 minutes and then serve with a side of your choice.

Smoked Haddock Penne

Makes 4 Servings.

Ingredients

3 cups of whole-wheat penne pasta

2 courgettes, chopped

5 stalks of asparagus, ends removed and chopped

1 cup of low fat crème fraiche

1 tbsp dill, finely chopped

2 fillets of smoked haddock, cut into small pieces

4 tbsp parmesan, freshly grated

Directions

Preheat your oven to 350F.

Bring a pot of water to the boil then add the pasta, courgettes and asparagus. Cook for 3-4 minutes then drain.

Once drained return to the pot and add the crème fraiche and dill. Stir well over a medium heat.

Add the haddock and gently fold everything together.

Season with black pepper and continue to fold until everything is evenly mixed.

Sprinkle parmesan over the top then cover and place the pot in the oven for 15-20 minutes. Note that if your pot isn't oven proof you will need to transfer to a baking dish for this stage.

Fish Tacos

Makes 4 Servings.

Ingredients

4 cups of cabbage, thinly sliced

1 cup of chopped tomatoes

¼ of thinly sliced green onions

¼ cup chopped fresh cilantro

2 tbsp fresh lime juice

5 tsp olive oil, divided

1 lb. tilapia fillets

1 tsp chili powder

8 small (6") whole wheat tortillas

Directions

Mix the first 4 ingredients in a bowl, then add the lime juice and 1 tbsp of the oil. Toss everything well.

Place a pan over a medium-high heat and add the remaining oil.

Sprinkle the tilapia with the chili powder and then add to the pan. Cook for 3-5 minutes per side.

Remove the fish from the pan and chop into small pieces.

Add the cabbage mixture to the pan and cook over a medium heat for 2 minutes. Add the fish back to the pan and toss well. Take off the heat.

Warm the tortillas in the microwave and then serve the tortillas alongside the cabbage and fish mixture. Let people create their own tacos.

Tarragon Butter Halibut

Makes 2 Servings.

Ingredients

2 halibut fillets

2 tablespoons unsalted butter

2 tbsp tarragon

Directions

Preheat your broiler/grill.

Make 2 individual foil trays and then lay the fish, skin side up, on them.

Mix the butter and chopped tarragon together then coat the fillets with the mixture.

Broil for 4 minutes before flipping and broiling for a further 4-5 minutes.

When serving pour any juices from the foil package over the fish.

Shrimp Linguine

Makes 4 Servings.

Ingredients

6 oz. of whole wheat linguine

2 tbsp unsalted butter

1 lb. of large shrimp, peeled and deveined

6 cloves of garlic, minced

¼ tsp red pepper flakes

4 large tomatoes, chopped

3 tbsp parsley, chopped

1 tbsp lemon juice

Directions

Cook the linguine according to package instructions and drain.

As the pasta is cooking melt 2 tsp of butter in pan over a medium-high heat.

Add the shrimp to the pan and cook for 2 minutes per side. Take out the pan and set aside.

Put the garlic, pepper flakes and remaining butter in the pan, cook well for 30 seconds. Add the tomatoes and cook for 2 minutes stirring frequently.

Return the shrimp to the pan and cook for 1 minute. Add the pasta. Parsley, lemon juice and toss well.

Spicy Tilapia

Makes 2 Servings.

Ingredients

2 tilapia fillets

2 tsp olive oil

½ onion, finely chopped

1 clove of garlic, minced

1 green bell pepper, chopped

1 zucchini, thinly sliced

4 oz. large mushrooms, thinly sliced

Cajun seasoning, to taste

Ground cayenne pepper, to taste

1 lime, cut in half

Directions

Place a pan over a medium heat and add the olive oil.

Once the oil is heated add the onion, garlic and pepper. Cook for 4 minutes then add the zucchini, cook for a further 1 minute stirring frequently.

Add the sliced mushroom, mix everything together and cook for 2 minutes.

Sprinkle the Cajun spices over the tilapia and add to the pan, cook for 3-4 minutes then turn.

Squeeze the lime over the other side of the fish, sprinkle with the cayenne pepper then cover the pan and cook for another 3 minutes.

Shrimp Stir Fry

Makes 4 Servings.

Ingredients

1 bag of beansprouts

1 & ½ cups of broccoli florets

1 red pepper, chopped

1 green pepper, chopped

2 tbsp olive oil

1 lb. shrimp, peeled and deveined

2 tsp brown sugar

1 tsp ground ginger

1 cup of orange juice

¼ cup soy sauce

Directions

Place a pan or wok over a medium heat and add the oil.

Add the broccoli and peppers to the pan, cook for 4 minutes then add the shrimp. Stir everything together well and cook for 3-5 minutes.

Add all the remaining ingredients to the pan and toss well. Bring to the boil stirring frequently and then let simmer for 2-3 minutes.

Coconut Mussels

Makes 3-4 Servings.

Ingredients

2 lb. of mussels

1 tbsp olive oil

1 onion, chopped

1 Thai chili, chopped

3 tsp of minced ginger

1 & ½ tbsp ground curry powder

½ cup of chicken broth

1 can of coconut milk

1 stalk of lemongrass, chopped

Chopped cilantro

Lime wedges

Directions

If required, clean the mussels.

Place a pot over a medium heat and add the oil. Cook the onion in the oil for 5 minutes then add the chilli, ginger and curry powder. Stir everything together and continue to cook for 1-2 minutes.

Add the chicken broth to the pot and cook until it is reduced by half. Mix in the coconut milk and lemon grass then bring to the boil. Once it comes to a rolling boil turn the heat to low add the mussels and cover.

Cook for 5-7 minutes until the mussels are open. Discard any mussels that aren't open as these are dead and not safe to eat.

Serve the mussels in the coconut sauce.

Tuna Steak

Makes 4 Servings.

Ingredients

4 tuna steaks

¼ cup of orange juice

¼ cup of soy sauce

2 tbsp olive oil

1 tbsp lemon juice

2 tbsp chopped parsley

1 clove of garlic, minced

½ tsp of oregano

Ground black pepper, to taste

Directions

Add the orange juice, soy sauce, lemon juice, parsley, garlic, oregano, pepper and olive oil to a bowl, mix well.

Place the tuna steaks in the marinade and leave for 45 minutes.

Place a pan over a medium heat and add 2 tbsp of the marinade. Cook the tuna steaks for 4-5 minutes per side.

Serve with your favourite side dish.

Tuna Steak Skewers

Makes 2-3 Servings.

Ingredients

2 tuna steaks, chopped into chunks

1 tbsp olive oil

½ tsp thyme

Ground cayenne, to taste

Ground paprika, to taste

2 onions, roughly chopped

2 bell peppers, cut into thick chunks

6 cherry tomatoes

½ zucchini, cut into chunks

Ground black pepper, to taste

Skewers, soaked in water

Directions

In a bowl combine the oil, thyme and pepper. Mix well and then add the chopped tuna steak to this mixture and cover. Leave in the marinade for 20 minutes.

Whilst the tuna marinades preheat your broiler/grill.

Skewer the vegetables and tuna in an alternating fashion.

Season with pepper.

Place under the broiler/grill and cook for about 3-4 minutes per side.

DASH Side Dishes

Cauliflower Mash

Ingredients

1 cauliflower, chopped into florets, discard stem

1 tbsp of chilli pepper flakes

Ground black pepper, to taste

Directions

Put the florets into a microwave proof bowl and add 1" of water.

Cover and cook for 2 minutes on high power.

Drain the water from dish and blast again for 1 minute.

Add the pepper and chilli flakes then mash together with a fork.

Greens Veg

Ingredients

1 head of Broccoli, chopped into florets

1 cup of chopped green beans

1 cup of spinach, pressed

1 courgette chopped

1 tbsp of minced garlic

½ tbsp cayenne pepper

2 tbsp olive oil

Ground black pepper, to taste

Directions

Put a pan over a medium and add heat the olive oil with the garlic.

Add the veg, except the spinach, and cook for 5 minutes, stirring frequently.

Sprinkle in the cayenne pepper. Cook for a further 2 minutes.

Throw in the spinach and cook until it wilts. Mix everything well.

Grind pepper over to season.

Ingredients

1 sweet potato, washed

1 tsp minced garlic

1 tsp ground paprika

1 tbsp olive oil

Directions

Preheat your oven to 350F

Pierce the sweet potato with a fork and microwave for 8-10 minutes.

Slice in half and pierce each face multiple times. Microwave for a further 5 minutes.

Cut halves again so you know have quarters.

Lay foil on a baking tray and place potato on it. Sprinkle with garlic and paprika then drizzle oil over everything.

Bake for 15 minutes.

Stuffed Mushrooms Caps

Ingredients

2 large cap mushrooms

¼ cup of tomato puree

½ cup of Goat's cheese, torn or crumbled

Ground black pepper, to taste

Directions

Preheat your oven to 350F.

Bake mushrooms for 5 minutes on a baking tray with underside facing up.

Take out of the oven and scoop out the flesh from the underside.

Add the mushroom flesh and tomato puree to the bowl, mix well. Generously season with black pepper.

Put the mixture back into the mushroom caps. Return to the oven for 6-7 minutes.

Sprinkle the goat's cheese on top and cook for a further 2 minutes.

Other Books by Sarah Sophia

The DASH Diet Chicken Cookbook: 30 Delicious Low Salt Chicken Recipes for Lowering Blood Pressure, Losing Weight and Improving Your Health

Baking Gluten Free Bread: Simple Recipes for Busy Moms

Gluten Free Italian: Simple and Delicious Recipes for Cooking Italian Cuisine

The Hot Sauce Book: Recipes for Making Your Own Hot Sauces and Cooking With Them

Green Smoothie Delight: Delicious Smoothie and Juice Recipes to Burn Fat, Improve Your Health and Feel Awesome

The Quinoa Cookbook: Quick, Easy and Healthy Recipes Using Natures Superfood

The Budget Cookbook: Cook Restaurant Quality Meals at Home on a Shoestring Budget

Printed in Great Britain
by Amazon